Getting the Job Done

How can we learn from everything we do?

page 4

page 18

THE GREAT ERASER

by Ilo Orleans

My blackboard was
The soft white sand,
Which stretched out far
On every hand.

I searched and found
An empty shell,
And wrote out words
That I can spell.

But waves dashed on
The sand to play,
And washed my letters
All away.

And that is how
I got the notion—
A great eraser
Is the ocean.

I Can Do It!

The child in "The Great Eraser" can write words in the sand. Remember when you first learned how to write? Writing takes time and practice, but now you can do it! Make an "I Can Do It!" display to show people some of the things you can do.

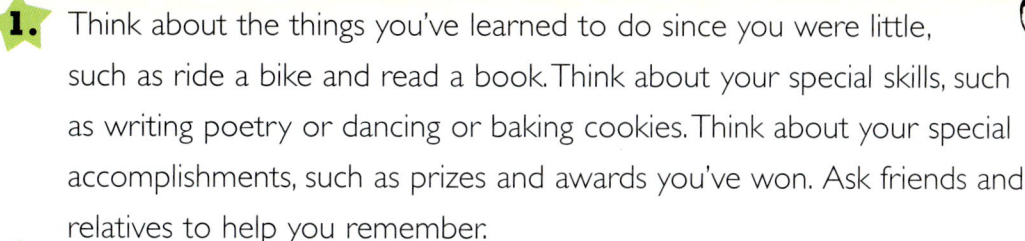

Gather Information

1. Think about the things you've learned to do since you were little, such as ride a bike and read a book. Think about your special skills, such as writing poetry or dancing or baking cookies. Think about your special accomplishments, such as prizes and awards you've won. Ask friends and relatives to help you remember.

2. Make a list of all these "I Can Do" things.

Organize and Draw Conclusions

3. Look over your list and number it. Ask yourself which things are most interesting and important to you.

4. Choose the top ten things on your list.

Write and Present

5. For each thing you chose, think of the most interesting way to tell about it. For example, let's say you have a dog that you take care of and train. You might:

• Tape a picture of your dog to the top of an index card and write about it.

• Put your dog's pawprints on a piece of paper and write about it.

• Write about your dog on a card and attach it to one of your dog's old toys.

• Draw and label pictures of you training your dog.

6. Make a display of your "I Can Do" things. You might tape them to a piece of tagboard or put them in a box. Share your display with the class.

7. What other new skills can you learn? As you learn how to do something new, add it to your display. See how many things you can learn!

Use What You Learn

8. Look at the cards and objects in your box. Think about what it takes to learn new skills and to reach your goals. Then write a "recipe" for success. Include at least five important "ingredients" for success.

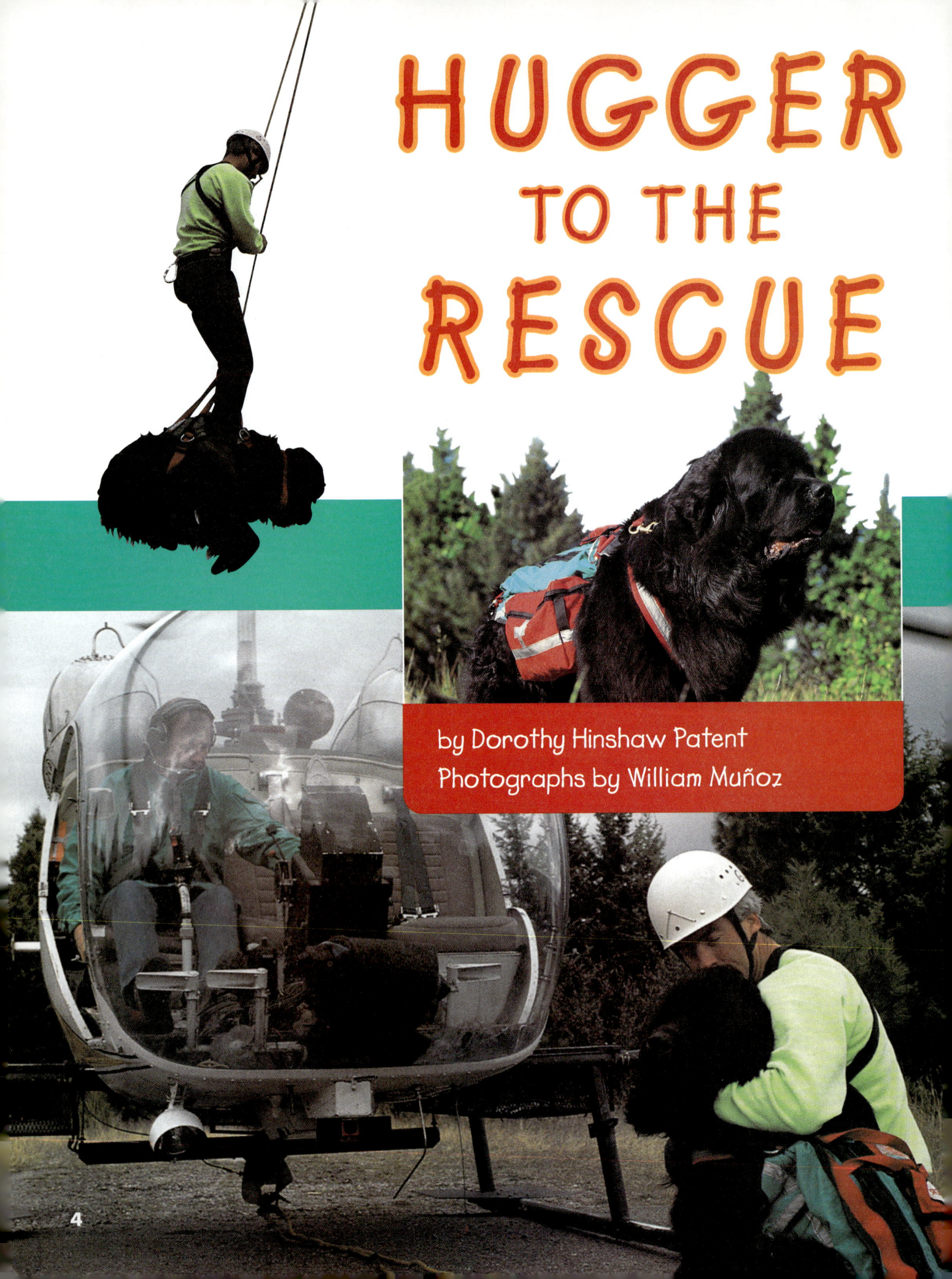

HUGGER
TO THE
RESCUE

by Dorothy Hinshaw Patent

Photographs by William Muñoz

Someone is lost in the woods. He might be hurt, or the weather could turn bad. It is important to find him as fast as possible. But he didn't follow a trail, and footprints don't show on the forest floor. What to do?

Call in search and rescue dogs. Dogs have a very fine sense of smell. They can find lost people by following their scents, because each person has his or her own, unique scent.

Panda and Susie are set to search for a person playing "lost" in a training session.

Panda sniffs the "lost" person's clothing.

She searches . . .

Panda is a Newfoundland dog trained to locate lost people. She and her owner, Susie Foley, know how to search through the woods, under the snow, or in the water. Sometimes a piece of the lost person's clothing is available for the dog to smell. But even without knowing the special scent, a trained dog knows to sniff the air, searching for the smell of a human.

Panda catches the scent and off she goes. She checks the ground if she loses the odor trail in the air. Once she finds the lost person, she licks him happily. Finding him is her best reward.

Search and rescue dogs work around the world to find lost hunters, hikers, and children. They are called in after avalanches to find people buried in the snow. After earthquakes,

finds the "victim," and shows him to Susie.

Dogs like Indigo can find avalanche victims in the snow quickly.

they look for people hidden in the rubble. Thousands of people owe their lives to these wonderful animals.

Many breeds of dogs are used for search and rescue. But most require a great deal of training to learn the work. Newfoundlands, however, are special. They have natural lifesaving instincts, so they learn their work quickly.

The Newfoundland — called a "Newfie" or "Newf" for short — originated on Newfoundland Island in Canada. It was developed as a working dog that performed a variety of tasks

Newfoundland puppies are born with the instinct to find lost people. They are natural swimmers and love the water.

like pulling carts and carrying heavy loads. The breed was most useful as a fisherman's companion, for Newfoundlands are as much at home in the water as on dry land. Their webbed feet help them swim, and their thick coats protect them from the icy cold of northern seas.

But saving people is the Newfie's greatest natural talent. Even without training, they will rescue people. During storms, Newfies may patrol the shore. When there have been shipwrecks, Newfies have rescued people without being trained to do so. Newfoundlands are famous for their rescuing skills, especially in water. They have carried lifelines to sinking ships and pulled countless drowning people to shore. A single untrained Newfoundland dog saved a hundred people in one

Hugger is big, even for a Newfie.

Susie Foley with Panda and Hugger

Newfies are gentle with children.

rescue. The water was too rough for rescue boats, but just one dog was able to do the job.

A dog has to be big to perform such work. Newfoundlands weigh from 100 to 160 pounds. They have heavy, muscular bodies and large heads. Most Newfoundlands are black. But they can also be brown, gray, or white and black. They are gentle, good-natured dogs that have a natural love for people.

Newfies make fine family pets. But such a huge dog is a big responsibility. It needs lots of food. A Newfoundland will eat twenty pounds of dry dog food each week, along with five pounds of meat. In addition, it can consume a pound of rawhide treats and two pounds of dog biscuits. Even with all that food, it will still enjoy table scraps and soup bones for chewing.

Chelsie is a good mother as well as a fine searcher.

Panda is always enthusiastic about her work.

Susie and Murphy Foley of Bigfork, Montana, raise and train Newfoundland dogs. Their animals are family pets that have a special job. Their volunteer organization, called "Black Paws Search, Rescue & Avalanche Dogs," has chapter groups sprinkled throughout the United States and in other countries. There are two good reasons for the name. Most Newfies do have black fur on their paws. But because of their love of wet places, all Newfoundlands are likely to have "black paws" any time they have a chance to get their feet muddy.

Susie and Murphy use several dogs in their work. Chelsie is a black female. She is loving and obedient, but she is also very determined to do things her way. When she finds a conscious victim, the searchers know right away because they can usually hear the person protesting her enthusiastic dog kisses.

Panda is white and black. Newfoundlands with this special color pattern are called "Landseers." Panda is huge, happy, and especially loyal to Susie. Only when she is at work looking for lost people does she willingly leave Susie's side.

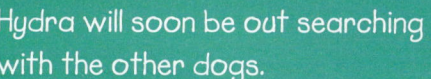
Hydra will soon be out searching with the other dogs.

Susie and Bill Weppler, Black Paws members, get ready to work with the dogs.

Hydra is just a puppy, but she is learning quickly how to become a fine search and rescue dog. She is curious and lively. Hydra acts as if she really wishes she could talk, she seems so eager to communicate with people.

Hugger, as his name suggests, is calm and lovable. He is especially eager to please, and his large size gives him extra strength that can come in handy in a challenging search. All these dogs, however, are really "huggers" — they love people and enjoy human companionship.

Even though they may rescue people without being taught, Newfoundland dogs need training. So do their human handlers. The dog must learn some important commands. The command "Wait" tells the dog to stop and wait for its handler to catch up — four legs work much better than two on rough or steep ground. If the dog gets distracted by wildlife or the tempting cool water of a creek, it must know to obey and get back to work when its handler calls out, "Leave it."

Puppies and older dogs enjoy one another's company.

At a very young age, Newfies become used to humans and their gadgets.

Meanwhile, the handler must get into top physical condition — searching is very hard work! He or she also needs to learn how to "read" the dog — how to know what the dog is trying to tell its handler. Each dog may have its own ways of "alerting" when it makes a find. The type of alert may vary, too, depending on whether the victim responds to the dog or not. For example, when Hugger finds a conscious victim, he wags his tail and waits to be invited over. But if the person is unresponsive, Hugger gives a "woof" while looking at Susie if she is nearby, then another woof. When he sees that she is coming to join him, he woofs one more time.

Training is best started when the dog is still young. Around eight weeks of age, a puppy is eager to learn and quite

Hydra gets her reward of loving attention for finding Sean during training.

Hugger is all ready to go.

unafraid of the unfamiliar. This is a good time to accustom it to situations that might be frightening later on. The puppy and its handler need to get acquainted by playing together, and cuddling creates a special bond. It is also important to become comfortable around other dogs.

Even a Newfie puppy knows how to follow a human scent and locate a person. It is important to give the puppy practice in searching and to reward success with plenty of praise and petting.

Black Paws' dogs must get used to wearing a uniform. The uniform is a very important part of their work. It carries first aid materials for both the dog and the victim, headlamps for work in the dark, dog cookies, and a canine energy drink.

Murphy helps Sooner cross a ravine using a rope. This is called "rappelling." Sooner is calm; he knows Murphy won't let him get hurt.

The uniform is an important piece of equipment. Harness straps are taken from their pockets when they are needed.

The uniform has a harness used when the animal needs to be hoisted by helicopter or rope. The harness straps are tucked into pockets on the uniform when not in use to keep them out of the way. When Susie puts a uniform on one of her dogs, it gets excited. It recognizes the call of duty.

The Newfies also need training for water rescue. They need to get used to riding in a boat and to signaling where a person is underwater when they catch the scent in the air. One way a dog can show the right spot is by leaning over and biting at the water. Then divers know to search in that spot.

Panda runs right to the spot where a person was buried in the snow in this training session. She digs right where the person's face is.

Being "found" by a Newfoundland means getting kissed.

For avalanche work, the dog needs to become used to riding on a chair lift which might be swaying in the wind. The dog must climb onto the lift willingly and ride calmly to the top. Once there, the dog has to search quickly. A person buried in the snow can suffocate or get dangerously cold very quickly.

Most search and rescue dogs need rewards like the chance to play ball or to eat a special treat, but not Newfies. Their reward is finding a person, saving a life. Their joy is obvious as they wag their tails and lick the faces of the people they rescue. No one wants to get lost in the woods or buried in the snow. But if it happens, there is no better way to be rescued than by a big, loving Newfoundland dog.

Just Add a Bark

Hugger is a Newfoundland dog. Did you know that an adult Newfoundland can weigh up to 160 pounds? Dogs come in many sizes. Look at the chart to see the "tall and short" of common breeds of dogs.

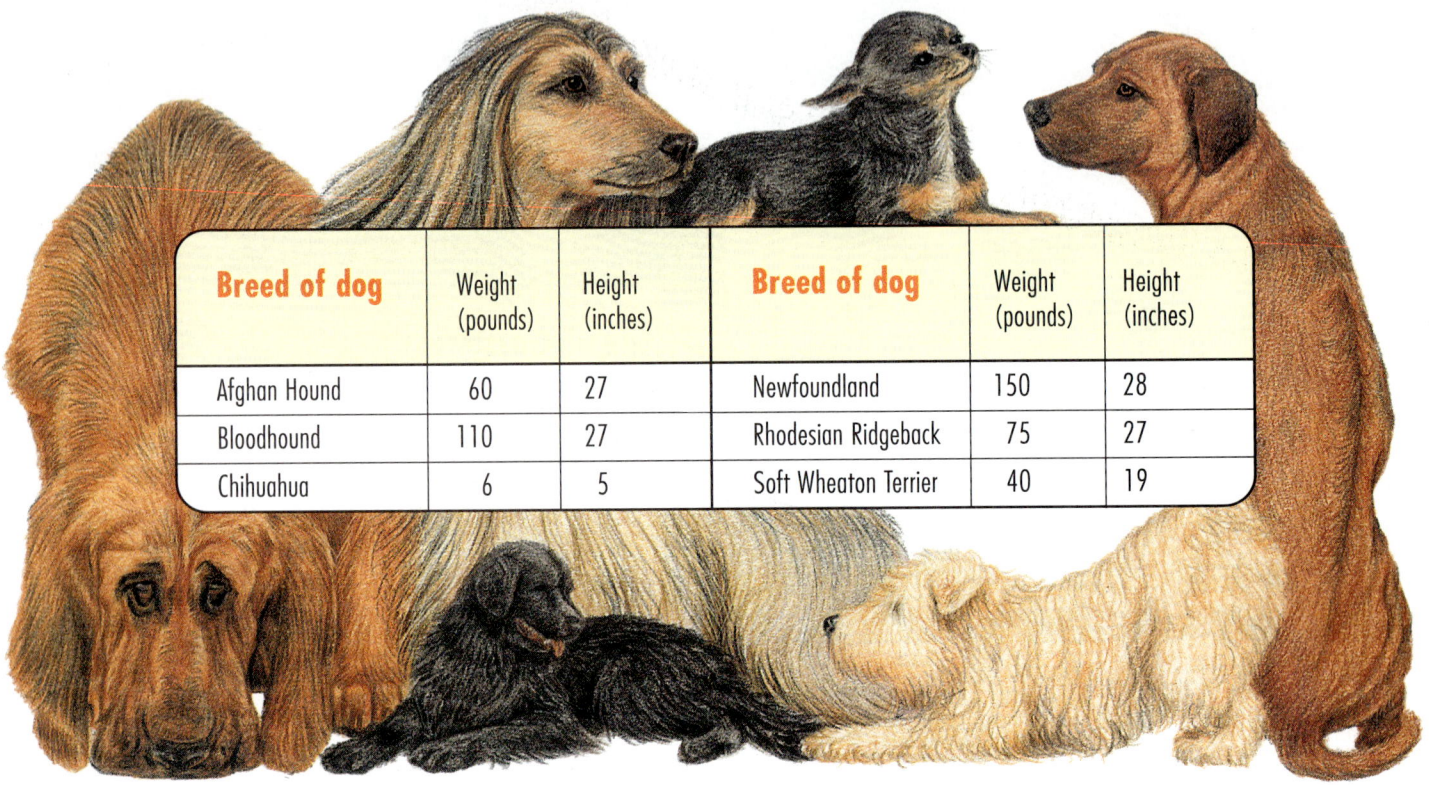

Breed of dog	Weight (pounds)	Height (inches)	Breed of dog	Weight (pounds)	Height (inches)
Afghan Hound	60	27	Newfoundland	150	28
Bloodhound	110	27	Rhodesian Ridgeback	75	27
Chihuahua	6	5	Soft Wheaton Terrier	40	19

Use measurements from the chart to work on some "doggy math."

What You Do

1. Make a bar graph to show the weights of the dogs. On the bottom of the graph, write the names of the dogs. On the left side of the graph, write a range of weights. Start with 0, and have each line stand for a multiple of 10 (10, 20, 30, and so on).

2. Make a second bar graph to show the differences in heights of the dogs. Again, write the names of the dogs on the bottom of the graph. On the left side, write a range of heights in inches. Start with 0 and have each line stand for a multiple of 2 (2, 4, 6, and so on).

Use What You Learn

3. Use your graphs to write two or more math problems about dogs. Exchange problems with classmates and solve them. Provide the answers too!

How to Care for Your CAT

Pet Care How-To

The Newfoundland dogs in *Hugger to the Rescue* need a lot of training and care. Newfoundlands eat 20 pounds of dry food and 5 pounds of meat each week, along with treats and dog biscuits. Rescue dogs also need rescue training and exercise every day.

Pets depend on owners to take care of their needs— shelter, exercise, food and water, cleaning, and playing.

What does it take to care for a pet? Make a pamphlet that shows how to take care of a pet of your choice.

What You Do

1. Choose a pet. You might choose a common pet, such as a cat or a hamster, or a more unique pet, such as an iguana or a ferret.

2. Find out how to care for the pet. You can use books or magazines, or you can ask questions at your local pet store or veterinarian's office. Focus your research on these questions:

- What kind of food does the pet eat? How much food and water does the pet need each day?
- What kind of shelter does the pet need?
- What kind of exercise does the pet need?
- What kind of training does the pet need? Can the owner train the pet, or does the pet need to go to special classes?
- Does the pet need to be groomed or cleaned? What kinds of tools are needed?

3. Use your information to make a pamphlet. Each section can discuss a separate part of the animal's care, such as food, exercise, toys, grooming, and so on. Include illustrations.

Use What You Learn

4. Look back at your pamphlet and ask yourself: What kind of person would be the perfect pet owner? Describe this person.

Rugby

& Rosie

by Nan Parson Rossiter

Rugby is my dog. He is a chocolate Labrador, and we have had him for as long as I can remember.

He walks with me to the school-bus stop in the morning, and he meets me there when I get home. He follows me around when I do my chores, and he sleeps beside my bed at night. He is my best friend.

We used to do everything together—just the two of us. Then Rosie came.

One fall day, my dad brought home a little yellow puppy. Her name was Rosie. She was so cute that I loved her right away. But she wasn't an ordinary puppy. She was coming to live with my family for only a year. Then Rosie would be old enough to go to a special school. There she would learn how to be a guide dog for a blind person. She and her new owner would always be together. They would be best friends. Just like Rugby and me.

I knew all this before Rosie came, but Rugby didn't. I held the puppy out to him to see how he would greet Rosie. She leaned forward eagerly and licked Rugby right on the nose.

Rugby gave one sniff and turned away. He made it very clear he wasn't interested in being friends.

"Come on, Rugby," I said. "She wants to play with you." And it was true. Rosie did want to play. But Rugby wasn't in the mood.

My mom and dad told me to be patient with Rugby, that he'd get used to having another dog around the house. But I wasn't sure. He looked so sad. Maybe he thought I didn't love him anymore, which wasn't true!

Rosie fit in with the family right away. She was so friendly and always wanted to play. She would chase after anything and then run back. She loved everyone in the

family—even Rugby! But he still wasn't friendly. Day after day, Rugby just moped around and wouldn't play with us.

That didn't bother Rosie one bit. She thought Rugby was the greatest. She trotted along after him, ran between his legs, tripped him, jumped on him, and barked at him.

Rugby did his best to ignore her.

But Rosie just wouldn't give up.

Then one day, Rugby was not waiting at the school-bus stop. I was worried. He *always* met me at the bus stop.

I ran home—and there I found Rugby asleep on the porch. Curled up in a little ball next to him was Rosie. "Rugby!" I said. They both looked up at me and wagged their tails. Rosie yawned and stretched and settled back down against Rugby's side.

From then on, Rugby and Rosie were always together.

They romped and played and chased the falling leaves. And they *both* waited for me at the bus stop.

Rosie was getting bigger. But she was still a puppy with lots of energy. Poor old Rugby tried his best to keep up! Soon winter came, and the three of us were racing and chasing through the new snow. We had so much fun together!

Sometimes it felt as if Rosie had always been with us—and always would be. I didn't want to think about the day when she would have to leave.

Rosie was old enough now for short lessons. Dad showed me how to teach her simple commands: *come, sit, stand, down, stay,* and *heel.*

We all worked to teach her good manners. A dog who begged for food at the table or jumped up on people would not make a good guide dog.

Rosie learned fast. Dad said that she was very smart and loved to please people. But she would have to pass many tests before she could become a guide dog.

I asked Dad what would happen if Rosie didn't pass the tests. He said that she couldn't be a guide dog, but she could still be a good pet. Then we would be able to keep her.

Now I didn't know what to think. I wanted Rosie to do well. I wanted to be proud of her. And I wanted her to help a blind person someday. I knew how important that was. But it was getting harder and harder to think of Rosie going away. And how could I explain it to Rugby? He loved Rosie as much as I did. Now the three of us were best friends.

When spring came, my family started taking Rosie on trips. We wanted her to be used to cars and buses and to the places where she would have to take her blind owner, like the bank and the store. We even took her to a restaurant. Of course, Rugby couldn't come with us. He always looked a little sad when Rosie got to go somewhere he couldn't go. And I knew he would be waiting for us when we got home.

Rosie would jump out of the car, and the two of them would race off, barking and playing and jumping. Later, they would come home in time for dinner, muddy and wet, with their tongues hanging out.

Soon summer came. The days were long and hot. Rosie was almost full grown. She was a beautiful dog. She and Rugby liked to sleep in the cool shade together. Sometimes the three of us went swimming in a nearby pond. Rugby and

Rosie loved to fetch sticks and tennis balls that I threw into the water.

It was a wonderful summer, and I wanted it to last forever. I knew that when fall came, it would be time for Rosie to go. When that day did come, I tried to be brave. Rugby and I stood and watched as Dad opened the car door for Rosie to jump in. Rugby wasn't upset. He didn't know that Rosie wasn't coming back. But I was so sad. I took Rugby on a long walk and tried not to think about Rosie. It was just like old times, before she came—when there were just the two of us.

When Dad came home, Rugby was waiting, his tail wagging. But, of course, Rosie wasn't in the car. Rugby looked all over for her. He whined. I wanted to explain everything, but I knew he couldn't understand. Instead, I buried my face in his neck and whispered, "She's gone, and I miss her too."

We all missed Rosie very much, especially Rugby. Her trainers called several times. At first, I hoped that Rosie wasn't doing well. Then she could come back to live with us. But the trainers said that she was doing fine and would

graduate with her new owner soon. That made me feel so mixed-up. I didn't want to think about Rosie with a new owner, but I knew how important Rosie would be to a person who needed her. Could that person love her as much as Rugby and I had?

I wanted to go to the graduation and see Rosie again. Then I had a great idea. I asked Dad if we could take Rugby too. I knew how he'd missed Rosie—after all, they'd been best friends.

We got special permission for Rugby to go to the graduation. I could hardly wait.

At the graduation, there were lots of people and dogs. Rugby spotted Rosie right away. She was in her guide-dog

harness, standing beside her new owner. She seemed so calm, and we thought she looked so proud. Rugby bounded over to her, pulling me along. The two dogs greeted each other nose to nose, tails wagging. But Rosie would not leave her owner's side. She was a working dog now with an important job to do.

Her owner talked to us for a while. She told us how grateful she was to have Rosie and what a wonderful dog she

was. And she thanked us for taking good care of her while she was a puppy.

When it was time to go, we said good-bye to Rosie. Poor Rugby. On the way home in the car, I tried to make him feel better. I talked to him and patted him. I told him that her new owner loved her and would take good care of her.

The next morning, Rugby was still moping around when my dad left in the car. I was excited—and nervous too.

I knew where my dad was going.

When the car came back, I was waiting with Rugby. Dad got out. He had a wiggly little puppy in his arms. I knew I was holding on to Rugby too tightly—wishing, hoping. I wanted him to know that, because we had all loved Rosie so much, we had decided we would help raise another puppy that would be ours for a year.

Dad knelt down in front of Rugby. "Rugby," he said, "this is Blue."

And Rugby leaned forward and licked that little puppy right on the nose.

Working Animals Around the World

Rosie is a working dog. The United States is not the only country in which people get help from animals. Read on to find out things that animals do to help people in countries all around the world.

Falcons, birds of prey, are used to catch smaller birds in Saudi Arabia. The falcons' owners eat the small birds that their falcons catch for them.

Big-Footed Water Buffalo are large but gentle animals that pull carts and help in the grain fields of India, Southeast Asia, and southern China. They also work in the rice fields of Vietnam, Indonesia, and Japan.

Llamas carry loads in the Andes mountains in Bolivia. They can walk over the rough ground there.

Siberian Huskies are dogs that pull sleds in northern Canada. They can reach areas that cars cannot.

Elephants carry heavy loads and move objects with their trunks to help people who live in Sri Lanka.

Camels are used in India to work the wells that water the crops. The camels are especially useful in dry countries because the animals don't need much water.

Silkworms spin silk in China. The silk is used to make expensive and beautiful fabric.

Otters catch fish and eels for their owners in Bangladesh.

Think about all these animals and the work they do. Do you think it is fair for people to use animals to help them? Why or why not? How do you think people train animals to work for them? Write your thoughts and share them with the class.

What Did They Say?

As Rugby and Rosie wag their tails and bark and play together, they show each other how they feel and what they want to do. They communicate.

Other animals communicate. If a rattlesnake is afraid, it signals its fear by shaking its tail. Wolves howl to tell other pack members where they are. How do different animals communicate?

What You Need

•posterboard •old magazines •tape or paste •drawing materials

What You Do

1. Choose four different animals that interest you. Use encyclopedias or nonfiction books to find out how the animals communicate.

2. Present what you have learned about animal communication. Divide the top half of a posterboard into four sections. In each section, draw one of the animals you researched. Below each drawing, write a few sentences that tell how the animal communicates.

3. On the bottom half of the posterboard, paste or tape magazine pictures of people using facial expressions, such as a smile or a frown, and other "body language" to show their feelings. Below each cutout, write what you think the people are trying to communicate and why you think so.

Use What You Learn

4. How do facial expressions and body gestures help us understand people who speak different languages? How can people who speak different languages communicate and work together to solve a problem or to get a job done? Get together with classmates and discuss your ideas.

Reader Response

1 Think About the Theme

How can we learn from everything we do? What do the dogs in *Hugger to the Rescue* and *Rugby & Rosie* learn from humans? What do the humans learn about dogs? Make a list to answer each question.

2 Ask a Question

Imagine that you and the dogs in these two selections could communicate with words. What are some questions you might ask them? What kinds of answers might they give you? Write a short dialogue between yourself and one or two of these dogs.

3 Use New Vocabulary

Write down some new words you learned from reading these two selections. Think of situations where you might use these words in the future. List the words and situations and tell why you might use those words.

4 Make Connections

Think about the work that Hugger and Rosie do. Which dog do you think has a more difficult job to do? Why do you think so? Discuss or write out your answers.

5 Analyze

In *Hugger to the Rescue*, the author writes about what it takes to be a good rescue dog. What are some physical traits, such as size, that make a good rescue dog? What are some mental traits, such as courage? Make lists. Write a description of the ideal rescue dog. Include the traits you've listed.